MW00963675

PROBLEMS THAT HIT HOME

AUTHOR
Lyman Coleman

PROJECT ENGINEER
Matthew Lockhart

CONTRIBUTORS
Jeff Coleman, Richard Guy

TYPESETTING
Sharon Penington

COVER DESIGN
Erika Tiepel

Photo on cover and repeated throughout book:
© 1994, Roy Morsch/Stock Market , Inc.

Scripture taken from
Today's English Version
Second Edition © 1992
Old Testament:
© American Bible Society 1976, 1992
New Testament :
© American Bible Society 1966, 1971, 1976, 1992
Published by
Thomas Nelson Publishers
Used by permission.

Seven Sessions on Family and Dating

Session	Bible Story	Team Building Goal
1 HEADACHES	Wedding in Cana/John 2:1-10	Team Sign Up
2 FAMILY FLARE-UPS	Prodigal Son/Luke 15:11-32	Learning to Share
3 FRIENDLY FIRE	Forgiveness/Matthew 18:21-35	Going Deeper
4 THE DATING GAME	Abram & Lot/Genesis 13:1-13	Affirmation
5 MAKING IT RIGHT	Anger/Matthew 5:21-26	Getting Personal
6 THE GOD OF SURPRISES	Emmaus/Luke 25:13-35	Learning to Care
7 HIGH OCTANE LOVE	Love Chapter/1 Corinthians 13	Team Celebration

SERENDIPITY HOUSE / Box 1012 / Littleton, CO 80160 / TOLL FREE 1-800-525-9563

COACH'S BOX - BEHIND THE SCENES

"Serendipity is the facility of making happy, chance discoveries."

Horace Walpole, 1743

Horace Walpole, the great English storyteller, coined the word "serendipity" to describe what happened to three princes from the island of Sherri Lanka who experienced one surprise after another on a trip—totally unexpected. The "serendipity" in this program is the surprise that happens when you get together around a common cause and work together as a team to accomplish something . . . . together. Every session has a step-by-step process for team building, starting off with fun crowd breakers and communication games and ending up with shared prayer and caring. Here's a bird's eye view of the overall team-building design. Note how the "disclosure" level gradually flows from session to session.

GROUP AGENDA

PROGRESS REPORT

SESSION 1
Team Sign Up.
Orientation. What's it all about.
How it works. Make a commitment.

Check In Examination.
Pinpoint where you are at the beginning of this program - page 3.

SESSION 2
Learning To Share.
Tell us a little about yourself. Who are you? Where are you from?

How's It Going?
What do you think about this program? On the disclosure scale - no risk.

SESSION 3
Going Deeper.
Tell us more about yourself. Your values. Your lifestyle. Why you do what you do?

How Do You Feel About Your Team?
What's the trust level? On the disclosure scale - low risk.

SESSION 4
Affirmation.
Let us tell you what we have observed about you so far. What we appreciate about you.

Where Have You Improved?
Take the Progress Report on page 3 again. On the disclosure scale - moderate risk.

SESSION 5
Getting Personal.
Tell us about your concerns.
Struggles. Hopes. Dreams

How Can We Help You in Prayer?
Learning how to pray. To be there for each other.

SESSION 6
Learning To Care.
Tell us what God is saying to you.
About your life. Your future.

How Can We Support You?
Learning how to minister to one another.

SESSION 7
Team Celebration.
Evaluate your experience. Let us tell you the contribution you made to the team.

What Happened To You?
Take the Progress Report on page 3 again to pinpoint your growth.

Progress Report

Check to see where you are three times during this course. . . .at the end of the. . . .

- First session
- Fourth session
- Seventh session

If you had a complete physical, mental, relational and spiritual check up at the Mayo Clinic by doctors in these fields, what would they conclude about you. Record your pulse in each of these areas by putting a dot on the line below to indicate how you see yourself—1 being POOR and 10 being EXCELLENT health.

PHYSICALLY: I am feeling good physically. I stay in shape. Exercise regularly. Eat right. Sleep well. Enjoy life. Physically, I am. . .

Poor ———————————————— Excellent
1 2 3 4 5 6 7 8 9 10

MENTALLY: I am feeling good about myself. I build myself up. I have some God-given abilities. Strengths. I like who I am. Mentally, I am. . .

Poor ———————————————— Excellent
1 2 3 4 5 6 7 8 9 10

RELATIONALLY: I am feeling good about sharing myself with others. I make friends well. Deal with conflict. Reach out. Care. Forgive. Relationally, I am. . .

Poor ———————————————— Excellent
1 2 3 4 5 6 7 8 9 10

SPIRITUALLY: I am feeling good about my relationship with God. I am getting my spiritual life together, putting God first. Spiritually, I am. . .

Poor ———————————————— Excellent
1 2 3 4 5 6 7 8 9 10

Love the Lord your God with all your heart,
with all your soul. . .with all your mind,
and with all your strength. . .and
Love your neighbor as you love yourself.
Mark 12:30-31

SESSION 1 - COACH'S BOX

This course has two goals: (1) Spiritual formation/content, and (2) Spiritual experience/group building. Check this box at the beginning of each session for the group building plan for the session.

GAME PLAN: Team Sign Up. By the end of this session, the group will know what this course is all about and be ready to make a commitment for the next six sessions. . .to be on the team. The content for this session is "no risk" on the disclosure scale.

> ON THE DISCLOSURE SCALE: Session 1.
> No Risk___x_____High Risk

AGENDA/FORMAT: Four parts to the meeting. Chairs are rearranged for each step in the agenda.

STEP 1:	STEP 2:	STEP 3:	STEP 4:
Crowd Breaker	**Warm Up**	**Bible Study**	**Caring**
All together or	Groups of 2	Groups of 4	Teams of 8
Teams of 8	15 minutes	15-30 minutes	15-20 minutes
15 minutes			

TEAMWORK:
There is a method to the madness for these group sizes. Read the "Word to the Youth Leader" on page 46. First, make sure the entire youth group is committed to this program. In this session, the goal is to form into sub-teams of eight and agree to the guidelines. If your youth group is not more than ten or twelve, you may want to keep the whole group together. If you have more than twelve, we recommend sub-dividing into teams of eight—with an adult or older youth in each sub-team. (*Again, reread the rationale on page 46*). Follow the instructions in the margin. Trust us, there is method to the madness.

CROWD BREAKERS/15 Minutes. (Time for only one crowd breaker is planned for in the session, so choose your favorite.)

Transportation
How many in your group? Divide that by two and subtract one. The object is to transport the whole group with only that number of limbs (arms or legs) touching the ground. The group has to travel as a unit from one side of the room to the other (about 10 yards) without falling apart. If that was too easy, try it again, subtracting two or three.

Suitcase Relay
Divide the group into equal teams—as many boys as girls. Give each team a suitcase. In each suitcase is a lady's dress and a man's suit—complete with shirt and tie. On the word GO, a first couple (boy and girl) from each team must run with their suitcase to the opposite end of the room, open the suitcase, and put on everything in the suitcase—the boy putting on the lady's dress and the girl putting on the man's suit. Then they carry their suitcase back to the starting line. Undress. Put the clothes back into the suitcase and hand the suitcase to the next couple. The first team to complete the relay wins.

LEADER:
ore you start, read A
rd to the Youth
ders, on page 46.

SESSION 1
Headaches

WARM UP
Groups of 2
15 minutes

LEADER:
s out books. Explain
mwork principle. Ex-
in diagrams on page
and theory behind 2's,
and 8's. Break into
ms of 8's. Then, pair
in 2's for Warm Up.
d Introduction and
time after 15 minutes
move to the Bible
y.

Headache Survey

Introduction. Welcome to the team. Your youth leader has probably explained what this course is all about. And the importance of teamwork in this program.

The program works like a sports training camp. In each session you will be put through a series of group-building exercises, starting out with groups of 2, then groups of 4 and finally a group of 8.

Over the time that you are in this course, you will have a chance to get to know each other real well. . .and learn how to help each other as a team.

To get started, your youth leader is going to help you pair off with one other person and work on the headache survey below. For each headache, decide together whether the situation is a 1-aspirin, 2-aspirin or a 3-aspirin headache. Then, discuss the questions at the bottom.

___ schoolwork
___ curfew/rules at home
___ braces
___ Sunday School/religion class
___ girls/boys
___ losing my driver's license
___ getting into college
___ arguing with my parents
___ not having a date for the prom
___ neighborhood games
___ people I don't get along with at school
___ worrying about my parent's getting divorced
___ network difficulties during favorite TV program
___ having someone you have confided in break your confidences and tell everyone

___ not having enough money
___ getting fat
___ death of a friend
___ grades
___ getting a job
___ getting up in the morning
___ fighting with parents about my music
___ nobody calls
___ sitting alone in school cafeteria
___ moving to a new school
___ wondering which friends are really friends
___ worrying about getting caught for something I did wrong
___ losing your boy/girlfriend to your best friend
___ violence at school
___ death of one or both of my parents

FEEDBACK: What did you learn about each other in this survey? Finish the two sentences about your partner.

1. We are a lot alike in our attitude about. . .

2. I would like to hear more about your attitude about. . .

LEADER:
Put two 2's together to make 4's. Rearrange chairs. Read Introduction and scripture aloud. Save 30 minutes for last part—Caring.

The Punch Bowl Incident

Introduction. The Bible study in this course is a little different from the usual Bible study because the purpose of this course is different. The purpose of this course is to become a Christian community in which you can talk about the real issues in your life with trust and respect for one another.

The Bible study is designed around a two-part questionnaire: (1) **Looking Into The Story**—about a story of someone in the Bible, and (2) **My Own Story**—about your own life. The questionnaire has multiple-choice options— and there is no right or wrong answer, because the purpose is not to test your knowledge of the Bible.

For this kick-off session, you will study a familiar story in the Bible about a wedding in Cana where Jesus turned water into wine. If you have seen the movie, *Fiddler on the Roof* you will appreciate the headaches in this story. Jewish weddings were big occasions. The whole community was invited. And wine was very important. When the wine ran out, it was a major problem.

We recommend that you discuss this story in groups of 4 because it is easier to discuss things when you are in a smaller group—and you can finish the discussion in 30 minutes.

Be sure to save the last 30 minutes in this session to regather with your team and make some important decisions about this course. Now, listen to the Bible story. Then, quickly move into groups of 4 and discuss the questionnaire below.

THE WEDDING IN CANA

Two days later there was a wedding in the town of Cana in Galilee. Jesus' mother was there, ²and Jesus and his disciples had also been invited to the wedding. ³When the wine had given out, Jesus' mother said to him, "They are out of wine."

⁴"You must not tell me what to do," Jesus replied. "My time has not yet come."

⁶The Jews have rules about ritual washing, and for this purpose six stone water jars were there, each one large enough to hold between twenty and thirty gallons. ⁷Jesus said to the servants, "Fill these jars with water." They filled them to the brim, ⁸and then he told them, "Now draw some water out and take it to the man in charge of the feast." They took him the water, ⁹which now had turned into wine, and he tasted it. He did not know where this wine had come from (but, of course, the servants who had drawn out the water knew); so he called the bridegroom ¹⁰and said to him, "Everyone else serves the best wine first, and after the guests have drunk a lot, he serves the ordinary wine. But you have kept the best wine until now!"

John 2:1-10

Looking Into The Story: In groups of 4, let one person answer question #1. The next person answer question #2, etc. . .through the four questions. Remember, there are no right or wrong answers. . .so speak up.

1. If you were the social editor for the local newspaper, what headline would you give this story?
   a. mother of preacher takes charge at wedding
   b. mother saves bridegroom from embarrassment
   c. wedding guests get drunk on new wine
   d. police investigating DUI scandal at wedding
   e. bridegroom can't explain about wine
   f. rumor that someone tampered with the punch bowl

2. Why do you think Jesus went to the wedding?
   a. his mother made him
   b. weddings are always fun
   c. the whole village was invited
   d. to perform a miracle

3. Why do you think Jesus' mother called on Jesus to do something about the wine problem?
   a. mothers are that way
   b. she was on the refreshment committee
   c. she wanted to save the bridegroom any embarrassment
   d. she wanted to show what her son could do

4. If you had been the bridegroom, how would you have felt when you heard about the new wine?
   a. relieved—I can't forget about the guests
   b. curious—how did this happen
   c. amazed—this is a miracle
   d. he probably had other things on his mind
   e. he was out of it

My Own Story: Note the change in the way you are to share. Go around your group on question #1. Then, go around again on question #2, etc. through the questions. Be sure to save the last 30 minutes for the Caring Time—to make some big decisions.

1. If your mother showed up at your meeting right now, what would you do?
   a. die on the spot
   b. leave
   c. be thrilled
   d. hope she would be quiet
   e. wonder why

2. What is the most exciting thing that is going on in your life right now?
   a. being in love
   b. being on the team at school
   c. running around with friends
   d. getting to know God personally
   e. belonging to a real Christian fellowship
   f. discovering my independence
   g. other:_____

3. What area in your life right now is giving you a few headaches?
   a. school: grades, teachers, stress, violence
   b. parents: expectations, communication
   c. church: having to go, to conform
   d. friends: getting along/losing some
   e. dating: getting serious, getting hurt
   f. God: my faith struggles
   g. future: what am I going to do with my life?

4. How do you feel about opening up and talking this way about yourself?
   a. strange—really strange
   b. fine—no problem
   c. awkward—what am I getting into
   d. thrilled—I love this stuff
   e. ask me next week—I'm not committing myself

5. Frankly, if you were going to commit to this program in personal growth, what would you want understood from the outset?
   a. I can say "I pass" anytime I want
   b. anything that is said in the session is strictly confidential—not to be repeated outside the room
   c. I'm not really into church—don't push religion on me
   d. I was in a group like this once and it scared me
   e. I'll commit only if the rest of the group is going to take this seriously— I'm tired of phony Christians

CARING
Teams of 8
15-20 minutes

LEADER:
If you have more than ten to twelve, form groups of 8 by bringing two groups of 4 together. This group of 8 will stay together for the rest of this program— and meet together at the beginning and at the close of each session.

Team Sign Up

Introduction: Now is the time to decide what you want to get out of this course. For yourself. Your team. And to agree on the ground rules for team-work. Follow these four steps.

Step 1: Check in. Turn to page 3 and let everyone on your team explain where you are right now on these areas of your life. (You will have a chance to retake this test at the close of the course to see where you have changed).

Step 2: Expectations. Give everyone a chance to share the top two things you would like to get out of this course, using the list below:

____ to have fun
____ to talk about the real stuff in my life
____ to get to know the Bible
____ to get closer as a youth group
____ to go out and do something
____ to reach out to other kids at school
____ to grow in my faith
____ hanging out with my friends
____ other:_____

Step 3: Ground Rules. What are one or two things on the list below that you would like to include in the ground rules for being in this course? See if you can agree on these?

_____ ATTENDANCE: I will be at the meetings for the six sessions except in case of emergency.

_____CONFIDENTIALITY: I will keep anything that is said at the meetings in confidence.

_____PRAYER: I will pray for the others on this team.

_____REACH OUT: I will invite others from school and church to join our group.

_____MISSION PROJECT: I would like to see our team commit to a mission project at the close of this course.

_____PARTY: I would like to see us celebrate this course together at the close with a party or retreat.

_____ACCOUNTABILITY: I would like to see us report in each week on our spiritual walk with Christ.

LEADER: the close of this ses- n, bring all of the ms together to rein- ce the commitment—to present every session.

Step 4: Prayer Partner. Inside of your team, choose one or two others to conclude this meeting. . .and every meeting for the next six sessions. . .with a time of prayer. Before you pray, "report" on how you are feeling. . .and where you want your prayer partner to pray for you this week. THEN, CALL DURING THE WEEK TO ASK "HOW'S IT GOING?"

SESSION 2 - COACH'S BOX

GAME PLAN: Learning to Share. By the end of this session, the group will be underway and ready for a progress report. How's It Going? Tell us what you think about the program. The content for this session is "low risk" on the disclosure scale.

ON THE DISCLOSURE SCALE: Session 2
No Risk_____x_____High Risk

AGENDA/FORMAT: Four parts to the meeting. Chairs are rearranged for each step in the agenda.

STEP 1: **Crowd Breaker** All together or Teams of 8 15 minutes	STEP 2: **Warm Up** Groups of 2 15 minutes	STEP 3: **Bible Study** Groups of 4 15-30 minutes	STEP 4: **Caring** Teams of 8 15-20 minutes

TEAMWORK:
There is a method to the madness for these group sizes. Read the "Word to the Youth Leader" on page 46. Make sure the entire youth group is committed to this program. In this session, the goal is to build upon the team concept layed out in Session 1. If your youth group is not more than ten or twelve, you may want to keep the whole group together. If you have more than twelve, we recommend sub-dividing into teams of six to eight—with an adult or older youth in each sub-team. Follow the instructions in the margin.

CROWD BREAKERS/15 Minutes.

Bigger and Better Hunt
Here's a scavenger hunt based on gaining weight. Divide into groups of four or six and give each group a small item such as a piece of string, a button or a cotton ball. Each team goes door to door in your neighborhood, exchanging its item for something bigger and better. For example, if you start with a button, you might exchange it for a jar, then a shoe box, than an old chair and so on.
The team returning with the biggest and best item wins.*

The Last Straw
Needed: a straw for each individual and two pieces of tissue paper. In this relay game each team lines up with their straws. The first person in line sucks up the tissue paper on the end of his straw and keeps it there by inhaling. He then gives it to the next person in line. Hands cannot be used. The game continues down the line till the last person has it on the end of his straw. Any time the tissue paper is touched or falls to the ground, it has to go back to the previous player.*

*Reprinted with permission of Group Publishing.

SESSION 2
Family Flare-Ups

WARM UP
Groups of 2
15 minutes

LEADER:
ap the last session.
eat the teamwork
ciples. Ask teams of 8
ivide into 2's—not the
e person as last ses-
.

Down Memory Lane

Introduction. In the last session, you made a commitment to be part of a team effort and you agreed on the ground rules for your team. Now, you are ready to start the process of becoming a team.

To get started, get together with one other person from your team and take a walk down memory lane. One of you answer the first question. Your partner take the next question, etc. . . . through the list.

If you have time left over, respond to what your partner said by finishing the half-finished sentences at the bottom under FEEDBACK.

Now, one of you start out by talking about #1.

I REMEMBER. . . .

1. My favorite TV program when I was in grade school. . .

2. My best subject in grade school. . .

3. My first pet. . .

4. The chore I hated to do. . .

5. My first big trip or vacation. . .

6. My favorite room in the house. . .

7. The time I got lost. . .

8. The fun thing we did as a family when I was in grade school. . .

9. The person who helped me with my homework. . .

10. The first thing I can remember wanting to be when I grow up was. . .

11. My hero at age 7. . .

12. The tower of strength in my family. . .

13. My favorite uncle or aunt. . .

14. My mother's favorite food or dessert. . .

15. The best Christmas present I ever received. . .

FEEDBACK:

1. I appreciate what you said about. . .

2. Your family reminds me of the movie. . .

11

LEADER
Combine two 2's to make
4's. Read Introduction
and scripture. Call time
20 minutes before closing
time.

Comeback Player of the Year

Introduction. To answer some of his critics who thought he was running around with the wrong people, Jesus told a story about a wayward son and a father that threw a party for this son when he came home.

As you listen to this familiar story again, try to put yourself in the situation of all three characters: the father, the younger brother, and the older brother. Then, move into groups of four and discuss the questionnaire. Remember, there are no right or wrong answers, so don't be afraid to speak up.

Be sure to save the last 20 minutes at the close to get back together with your team for the caring time.

THE LOST SON

¹¹Jesus went on to say, "There was once a man who had two sons. ¹²The younger one said to him, 'Father, give me my share of the property now.' So the man divided his property between his two sons. ¹³After a few days the younger son sold his part of the property and left home with the money. He went to a country far away, where he wasted his money in reckless living. ¹⁴He spent everything he had. Then a severe famine spread over that country, and he was left without a thing. ¹⁵So he went to work for one of the citizens of that country, who sent him out to his farm to take care of the pigs. ¹⁶He wished he could fill himself with the bean pods the pigs ate, but no one gave him anything to eat. ¹⁷At last he came to his senses and said, 'All my father's hired workers have more than they can eat, and here I am about to starve! ¹⁸I will get up and go to my father and say, "Father, I have sinned against God and against you. ¹⁹I am no longer fit to be called your son; treat me as one of your hired workers."' ²⁰So he got up and started back to his father.

"He was still a long way from home when his father saw him; his heart was filled with pity, and he ran, threw his arms around his son, and kissed him. ²¹'Father,' the son said, 'I have sinned against God and against you. I am no longer fit to be called your son..' ²²But the father called to his servants. 'Hurry!' he said, 'Bring the best robe and put it on him. Put a ring on his finger and shoes on his feet. ²³Then go and get the prize calf and kill it, and let us celebrate with a feast! ²⁴For this son of mine was dead, but now he is alive; he was lost, but now he has been found.' And so the feasting began.

²⁵"In the meantime the older son was out in the field. On his way back, when he came close to the house, he heard the music and dancing. ²⁶So he called one of the servants and asked him, 'What's going on?' ²⁷'Your brother has come back home,' the servant answered, 'and your father has killed the prize calf, because he got him back safe and sound.' ²⁸The older brother was so angry that he would not go into the house; so his father came out and begged him to come in. ²⁹But he spoke back to his father, 'Look, all these years I have worked for you like a slave, and I have never disobeyed your orders. What have you given me? Not even a goat for me to have a feast with my friends! ³⁰But this son of yours wasted all your property on prostitutes, and when he comes back home, you kill the prize calf for him!' ³¹'My son,' the father answered, 'you are always here with me, and everything I have is yours. ³²But we had to celebrate and be happy, because your brother was dead, but now he is alive; he was lost, but now he has been found.' "

Luke 15:11-32

Looking Into The Story: In groups of 4, let one person answer question #1; the next person question #2, etc. through the four questions. If anyone wants to disagree, let them speak up.

1. Who does your heart go out to in this story?
   a. the father
   b. the older brother
   c. the prodigal son
   d. the pigs

2. Why do you think the prodigal son left home?
   a. to grow up
   b. to get away from his father's values
   c. he couldn't stand his older brother
   d. to try out forbidden things
   e. to try to make it on his own

3. Do you think the father should have given the youngest son the money?
   a. sure
   b. he had no choice
   c. maybe not
   d. absolutely not

4. If the father had a pretty good idea where his son went, do you think he should have gone after his son?
   a. yes, you don't want to see your kid get in trouble
   b. maybe, if he could get him to come home
   c. no, you've got to let the son make his own mistakes
   d. it all depends

5. What made the son come home?
   a. he got hungry
   b. he was homesick
   c. he wanted a place to sleep
   d. he felt sorry for his father
   e. he wanted to see his brother
   f. he realized that he had made a mistake

6. What do you think the prodigal son was feeling when he first saw his father again?
   a. scared—wanting to run again
   b. nostalgic—thinking of old times
   c. guilty—thinking how he had hurt his father
   d. loving—thinking how much he missed his dad
   e. defensive—thinking up excuses for what he had done
   f. calm—knowing he was doing the right thing

7. Do you think the father was wise in throwing a party for the prodigal son—and killing the fatted calf?
a. no, this was pure favoritism
b. maybe not, because of the older brother
c. no, because the prodigal son had done wrong
d. sure, because this is what love is all about

8. If you had been the older brother and saw your own inheritance being spent on a party for your little brother, how would you feel?
a. angry
b. confused
c. resentful
d. happy to see my brother home
e. let down

My Own Story: Note the shift in the sharing procedure. Go around your group on question #1 and let everyone answer. Then, go around on question #2, etc.

1. Where are you in the birth order in your family?
a. oldest
b. youngest
c. middle

2. Do you think where you are in the birth order in your family has made you more responsible or less responsible than your brothers/sisters?
a. more responsible
b. no effect
c. less responsible
d. I don't know

3. When there are hassles in your family, what usually is the reason?
a. grades
b. expectations
c. curfew
d. money
e. car
f. clothes
g. values
h. TV/music
i. church
j. friends
k. other:_____

4. In your family, how do you deal with conflicts?
a. my parents blow their top
b. I walk out
c. we try to talk it out
d. we go to a family counselor
e. my mom "sweeps it under the rug"
f. we are doing better

LEADER:
ing teams back togeth-
for Step 1 and 2. Then,
ep 3 with prayer part-
rs for this course.

Team Check-In: How's It Going?

Introduction: After two sessions in this program, stop the camera and evaluate what you think about the program. . .and what you would like to change.

Regather with your team and go over the questions together. Be sure to save the last few minutes to be with your prayer partner (Step 3).

Step 1: Check Your Pulse. What do you appreciate most about this course? Go around and let everyone share one or two things.

___ fun times
___ studying the Bible
___ close relationships
___ feeling like I belong
___ sharing our problems
___ praying for each other
___ reaching out to others
___ other:_____

Step 2: I Wish. If you could have one wish for this program, what would be your wish? Finish the sentence, I wish we could have. . .

___ more sharing about each other
___ more time for Bible Study
___ more fun
___ more reach out
___ more trips
___ less joking around
___ less gossip
___ less study
___ other:_____

Step 3: Prayer Partner. Get together with your prayer partner that you started with last week, and describe the last seven days in your life as a weather report. Then, close in prayer for each other. Finish the sentence, "This past week has been. . ."

❑ Blue sky, bright sunshine all week long—NO PROBLEMS
❑ Partly cloudy most of the week—A FEW PROBLEMS AT HOME
❑ Severe storms all week long
❑ mixed—some days sunny, some days cloudy
❑ warming trend—getting better
❑ tornado/hurricane—DISASTERS!
❑ other:_____

SESSION 3 - COACH'S BOX

GAME PLAN: Going Deeper. At the end of this session, the group will be asked to express how they feel about their group—whether they are "playing as a team" or "just looking on." On the disclosure scale, this session will be medium to low risk.

ON THE DISCLOSURE SCALE: Session 3
No Risk_____x_____High Risk

AGENDA/FORMAT: Four parts to the meeting. Chairs are rearranged for each step in the agenda.

STEP 1:	STEP 2:	STEP 3:	STEP 4:
Crowd Breaker	**Warm Up**	**Bible Study**	**Caring**
All together or	Groups of 2	Groups of 4	Teams of 8
Teams of 8	15 minutes	15 -30 minutes	15-20 minutes
15 minutes			

CROWD BREAKERS/15 minutes

Pictionary

A great game for leading into this study would be one like Pictionary where one team member is given the name of an object or concept that they must draw for their team on paper without using words, numbers or symbols. The first team to figure out the answer wins. You can use your own words or the cards from a Pictionary game. Play as many rounds as you want, or you can make the team member act out the concept, object or phrase. This gets them thinking about communication.

Co-ed Blanket Volleyball

This is wild fun! Play regular men's volleyball rules but cover the net with lightweight blankets, sheets or canvas so the opposing players cannot see each other or know where the ball is coming from.

Line Pull

Divide the group into two equal teams. The teams then face each other, by lining up on two sides of a line drawn on the floor. The object of the game is to pull the other team onto your side of the line. You cannot move behind your side of the line farther than three feet, and you must try to reach out and grab someone on the other side of the line without stepping over the line. Once you are over the line, you are automatically a member of that team and then you must try to help pull your former team over the line. At the end of the time period, the team with the largest number wins. This game can symbolize the pressure and pull of groups/gangs upon individuals. Being pulled across your personal lines of morality.

SESSION 3
Friendly Fire

Friendship Survey

Introduction. This session is about hassles among friends—what to do with conflicts. To get started, find one person that you have not been with before and discuss your preferences in choosing friends. On the first category—PERSONALITY—put a dot on the line somewhere in between the two extremes and explain to your partner. Then, let your partner explain where they put the dot and why. Then, move to the next category, etc. . . through the list. "For Friends, I would choose. . ."

PERSONALITY
Similar to mine _____different to me

COMMUNICATION
motor mouth _____quiet as a mouse

TEMPERAMENT
laid back _____intense

COMPATIBILITY
like doing the   not afraid to disagree
same things _____and go their own way

LOYALTY
go along with me   challenge me
through thick and thin_____when I need it

SELF ESTEEM
put themselves down   brag about themselves
all the time_____all the time

RELATIONSHIP TO THEIR FAMILY
speak highly   always complaining
of their parents _____about their parents

MORAL STANDARDS
wild and free _____stick to the rules

RELATIONSHIP TO A CHURCH
couldn't care less _____very committed

ATTITUDE ABOUT LIFE
optimistic_____pessimistic

How Many Times?

Introduction. Even among the closest of friends, sometimes we hurt each other. In the Bible study, the Apostle Peter asks Jesus what to do when you get hurt by a friend. He was probably talking about relationships within the close circle of friends in the followers of Christ.

Have someone read the story. Then, divide into groups of 4 and discuss the questionnaire. Remember, there are no right answers. . .so feel free to share.

THE PARABLE OF THE UNFORGIVING SERVANT

[21] Then Peter came to Jesus and asked, "Lord, if my brother keeps on sinning against me, how many times do I have to forgive him? Seven times?"

[22] "No, not seven times," answered Jesus, "but seventy times seven, [23] because the Kingdom of heaven is like this. Once there was a king who decided to check on his servants' accounts. [24] He had just begun to do so when one of them was brought in who owed him millions of dollars. [25] The servant did not have enough to pay his debt, so the king ordered him to be sold as a slave, with his wife and his children and all that he had, in order to pay the debt. [26] The servant fell on his knees before the king. 'Be patient with me,' he begged, 'and I will pay you everything!' [27] The king felt sorry for him, so he forgave him the debt and let him go.

[28] "Then the man went out and met one of his fellow servants who owed him a few dollars. He grabbed him and started choking him. 'Pay back what you owe me!' he said. [29] His fellow servant fell down and begged him, 'Be patient with me, and I will pay you back!' [30] But he refused; instead, he had him thrown into jail until he should pay the debt. [31] When the other servants saw what had happened, they were very upset and went to the king and told him everything. [32] So he called the servant in, 'You worthless slave!' he said. 'I forgave you the whole amount you owed me, just because you asked me to. [33] You should have had mercy on your fellow servant, just as I had mercy on you.' [34] The king was very angry, and he sent the servant to jail to be punished until he should pay back the whole amount."

[35] And Jesus concluded, "That is how my Father in heaven will treat every one of you unless you forgive your brother from your heart."   Matthew 18:21-35

Looking Into The Scripture. In groups of 4, let one person answer question #1, the next person question #2, etc.

1. In the Scripture, what is Peter really asking in his question?
   a. How much do I have to put up with my friends?
   b. Do I have the right to be ticked off?
   c. When my friend does not measure up to my expectations, what do I do?
   d. My friend makes me mad. Do I have the right to cut this person off?
   e. How can I live a moral life when I have to live with people who take advantage of me?

2. Why do you think Peter—the hot-headed disciple who was always flying off the handle—asked Jesus this question?

   a. he was the type to speak up when others kept quiet

   b. he couldn't bear to see broken relationships in their group go unforgiven

   c. he felt guilty because he couldn't get along with someone in the group who made him "blow his top"

3. What is Jesus really saying in the parable?

   a. You can't "keep score" of wrongs

   b. You've got to be as patient with your friend as God is with you

   c. If you are really a Christian you will not have conflicts.

   d. If you don't forgive your friend, you will be cast into the fire of hell

   e. If you have experienced God's forgiveness, you will be more patient with your friend

4. How do you think Peter felt when Jesus finished answering his question?

   a. worse

   b. this is going to be hard for me to do

   c. don't know what goes on with this Jesus

   d. I'm sorry I asked

   e. other:_____

My Own Story: Note the shift in the way to discuss the questions below. On question #1, everyone answer the question and explain why. Then, go around again on question #2, etc. . .through the questions.

1. What would you do in this situation? You hear by the grapevine that your close friend went to the basketball game with some kids without inviting you. You found out when you went to the game by yourself and discovered your friend sitting there with these kids. What would you do?

   a. ask if you could join them

   b. pretend that you didn't see them

   c. stare at your friend and look disappointed

   d. assume that your friend had a reason for not calling you

   e. forget the whole thing

   f. call your friend when you got home and have it out

2. What would you do? The word gets back to you that something you shared in confidence with your youth group last week is "all over school." What do you do?

   a. stop going to youth group

   b. confront the youth group and tell them how this hurt you

   c. never share anything again at the youth meetings

   d. go to the youth leaders/ask them to handle it

   e. go to the person that you think said it and have it out

   f. accept this as part of life and try to get on with it

3. When you get hurt in relationships, what do you do?
  a. have it out with the person
  b. sulk for three days
  c. withdraw into myself
  d. cry on my youth leader's shoulder
  e. try to look at it from the other person's point of view
  f. watch reruns all night
  g. complain to God

4. What is the easiest way for you to deal with conflict?
  a. write a letter
  b. stop communicating
  c. take the person out for a Coke
  d. surprise the person with a little gift
  e. ignore it and hope for the best
  f. be up front about it

5. In your youth group, how do you deal with conflicts?
  a. ignore them
  b. talk about them
  c. let the youth leader deal with the mess
  d. we don't have conflicts

How Do You Feel About Your Team?

Introduction: You have been together for three sessions. Take your pulse on how you feel about your group. Steps 1 and 2 are for your team together. Step 3 is with your prayer partner.

Step 1: Report In. If you could compare your involvement in this program to somewhere on the diagram below, where would you be:

- In the grandstand—for spectators—just looking on
- On the bench—on the team—but not playing
- On the playing field—where the action is
- In the showers—on the injury list

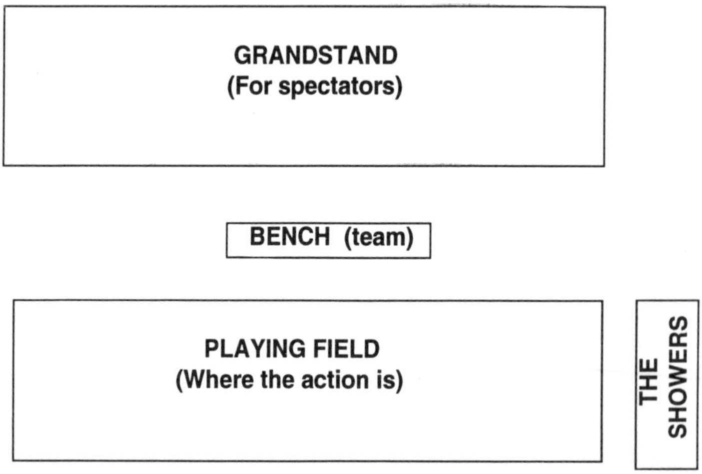

```
┌─────────────────────────────────────┐
│                                     │
│            GRANDSTAND               │
│          (For spectators)           │
│                                     │
└─────────────────────────────────────┘


            ┌──────────────────┐
            │  BENCH  (team)   │
            └──────────────────┘

┌──────────────────────────────────┐  ┌──────┐
│                                   │  │      │
│          PLAYING FIELD            │  │ THE  │
│        (Where the action is)      │  │SHOWERS│
│                                   │  │      │
└──────────────────────────────────┘  └──────┘
```

Step 2: Teamwork. How would you describe the way you work together as a team in sports language? Finish the sentence: When we play together we're. . .

- jittery—like in our first game
- learning to trust each person on the team
- awkward—but we're improving
- fourth and goal to go—let's get it done!

Step 3: Prayer Partner. Get together with your prayer partner for this program and check to see how it went last week. Then, spend a little time in prayer for each other. Start off by picking a number from 1 to 10—1 being TERRIBLE and 10 being GREAT—to describe how last week went.

SESSION 4 - COACH'S BOX

GAME PLAN: Affirmation. At the end of this session, the group will do two things: (1) Retake the Progress Report on page 3 and (2) Affirm each other for the contribution each person is making to the team. On the disclosure scale, this session will be medium risk.

ON THE DISCLOSURE SCALE: Session 4.
No Risk_____x_____High Risk

AGENDA/FORMAT: Four parts to the meeting. Chairs are rearranged for each step in the agenda.

STEP 1:	STEP 2:	STEP 3:	STEP 4:
Crowd Breaker	**Warm Up**	**Bible Study**	**Caring**
All together or	Groups of 2	Groups of 4	Teams of 8
Teams of 8	15 minutes	15-30 minutes	15-20 minutes
15 minutes			

CROWD BREAKER/15 Minutes.

Scavenger Hunt
   Equipment: Whatever is in your wallet, purse or pockets. This game is played like an "old-fashioned" scavenger hunt, except this time the teams have to produce the items from things they have in their possession. One person acts as the referee in the center of the room. Each team sits in a cluster (an equal distance) from the referee in the center. The referee calls out an item, such as a shoestring. . .and the first team to bring this item to the referee in the center of the room is the winner. Points are awarded to the team based on the "difficulty/factor" in obtaining the items. The referee keeps score and periodically announces the score. (If one team is ahead, the referee can equalize the score by awarding a few extra points for the next item.)
   Here is a list of items and suggested points or you can add your own items and point system. Call out one item at a time. For 1000 points, the first team to bring to the referee a:
   ❏ sock with a hole in it
   ❏ seal of the United States (dollar bill)
   ❏ baby picture
   ❏ something that smells
   ❏ guy with lipstick on
   ❏ love letter

For 2000 points, the first team to bring to the referee:
   ❏ three shirts on one person backwards and buttoned up
   ❏ three different colored hairs tied together
   ❏ four shoes that total 29 in shoe sizes. . .tied together

For 3000 points, the first team to bring to the referee:
   ❏ two people inside one shirt. . .all buttoned up
   ❏ one person with 4 belts, 3 shirts, and 8 socks on

For 5000 points, the first team to bring to the referee:
   ❏ the whole team surrounded by a rope made out of socks

SESSION 4
The Dating Game

This Is Your Life

Introduction. With this session, you reach the mid-point in this course on dealing with hassles. At the end of this session, you will have a chance to evaluate the first half.

This session is about hassles in dating relationships. To get started, get together with one other person that you have not been with before and interview each other for a feature story about your attitudes about dating for *People Magazine.* The interview questions to ask are below. If you have time left over, respond to your partner by finishing the two sentences below under FEEDBACK.

1. What is your "nickname"? What do your friends call you?

2. When you were seven years old, who was your hero?

3. Who was your first "true love"—the little boy or girl next door?

4. What TV show or movie did you like because it showed a dating relationship that you admired?

5. What TV show or movie did you not like because it showed dating relationships that were not attractive to you?

6. When it comes to dating, what do you look for in a date?

7. When it comes to going steady, what do you look for in a steady?

8. When it comes to marriage, what would you look for in a mate?

FEEDBACK: Respond to what your partner said by finishing these two sentences:

1. The way you look upon dating reminds me of the character in the movies or the TV show. . .

2. I wish we had more time to talk about your ideas about. . .

Conflict Resolution

Introduction. There are not a whole lot of stories in the Bible about dating relationships because there was not a whole lot of dating in Bible times. Marriages were arranged by the parents—like you see in the story of Abraham finding a wife for his son Isaac.

For this reason, we have chosen a story about a family hassle that could be applied to dating relationships—the story of the separation of Abraham and Lot. Here's the background to the story.

Abraham had a brother who died, and Abraham took on the responsibility of raising his brother's son, Lot. They went into business together—raising cattle. Before long, they got into a disagreement over grazing land. Listen to the story as it unfolds. Then, move into groups of four and discuss the principles involved here that apply to any close relationship—like dating.

Be sure to save the last 20 minutes at the close for the caring time.

ABRAM AND LOT SEPARATE

Abram went north out of Egypt to the southern part of Canaan with his wife and everything he owned, and Lot went with him. ²Abram was a very rich man, with sheep, goats, and cattle, as well as silver and gold. ³Then he left there and moved from place to place, going toward Bethel. He reached the place between Bethel and Ai where he had camped before ⁴and had built an altar. There he worshiped the Lord.

⁵Lot also had sheep, goats, and cattle, as well as his own family and servants. ⁶And so there was not enough pasture land for the two of them to stay together, because they had too many animals. ⁷So quarrels broke out between the men who took care of Abram's animals and those who took care of Lot's animals. (At that time, the Canaanites and the Perizzites were still living in the land.)

⁸Then Abram said to Lot, "We are relatives, and your men and my men shouldn't be quarreling. ⁹So let's separate. Choose any part of the land you want. You go one way, and I'll go the other."

¹⁰Lot looked around and saw that the whole Jordan Valley, all the way to Zoar, had plenty of water, like the Garden of the Lord or like the land of Egypt. (This was before the Lord had destroyed the cities of Sodom and Gomorrah.) ¹¹So Lot chose the whole Jordan Valley for himself and moved away toward the east. That is how the two men parted. ¹²Abram stayed in the land of Canaan, and Lot settled among the cities in the valley and camped near Sodom, ¹³whose people were wicked and sinned against the Lord.

Genesis 13:1-13

Looking Into The Story: In groups of 4, let one person answer question #1; the next person question #2, etc. Remember, there are no right or wrong answers. . .so feel free to express your opinion.

1. Which of these statements best express what Abram said about this conflict?
   a. "We've gotta solve this problem here and now. You take whatever you want and I'll be satisfied with what you don't take."
   b. "This is what we are going to do and don't try to change my mind."
   c. "Let's just play it cool and maybe this whole deal will blow over."
   d. "I value your friendship too much to let this dispute stand in the way."

2. What did Abram do by letting Lot have first choice?
   a. he took the initiative in solving the problem
   b. he forced Lot to make a decision
   c. he preserved their relationship
   d. he gave some space for the quarrel to go away

3. How do you think Lot felt when Abram did this?
   a. terrible
   b. ashamed
   c. delighted
   d. relieved
   e. wondering—why is he doing this

4. Sodom, where Lot eventually moved, had a really bad "red light district." Had Abram known about this, what do you think he should have done?
   a. warned his nephew
   b. decided to go there instead of his nephew
   c. gone there with Lot for a wild party, and forget about their conflict
   d. not worried about it, being confident in his brother's morality
   e. not cared—that was Lot's business

My Own Story: Start off by discussing the two CASE STUDIES. Then, share some of your own story.

CASE STUDY 1: Scott and Gwinn
   Scott and Gwinn had been going steady for two years when he received the shocking letter. She didn't love him anymore. "I don't think it is working out."
   Scott was deeply hurt. He withdrew into himself and "played it safe" in all his relationships. When his friends tried to reach out to him, he drew back. "I don't want to get burned. . .again."
   Scott has not gotten burned since then. . .but there is something missing in his life. If you had been Scott, what would you have done?

   a. the same thing
   b. had it out with Gwinn—face to face
   c. sent flowers and a kind note
   d. found someone else right away to take her place
   e. taken off for the mountains to be by yourself
   f. gotten drunk
   g. gone to a friend for advice

CASE STUDY 2: Bill and Sally

Bill and Sally are leaders of the youth group. They also have been going together for over a year. Then, something happened that they don't want to talk about. The youth group is feeling the pain of this broken relationship. The meetings are edgy. Sharing is shallow. And it is hard to pray together. Nobody wants to say anything for fear of offending Billy or Sally, but something must be done. What would you do?

    a. let the youth leader deal with it
    b. bring this up before the youth group
    c. privately, explain how the broken relationship has affected the group
    d. ask Bill and Sally to leave
    e. ask Bill to leave
    f. try to ignore it
    g. this has never happened in our youth group

REFLECTION: Go around the group on question #1. Let everyone give their answer. Then around on question #2, etc.

1. When you break up in a dating relationship (or go your separate ways), what do you do?
    a. don't talk to him/her
    b. feel guilty
    c. deliberately try to avoid him/her
    d. talk badly about them to others
    e. take it out on everybody else—especially my parents
    f. leave on a friendly note
    g. ask if there is anything I have done to hurt them
    h. leave the door open for continued friendship

2. If you are breaking off the relationship because of a moral issue, what would you do?
    a. be up front about it
    b. break off the relationship but not tell them why
    c. tell my friends why and hope the word gets back to them
    d. break off the relationship but try to keep the friendship
    e. disappear and not say why to anybody

3. If this person is a member of your youth group or a committed Christian, do you think you owe this person a little more consideration?
    a. no
    b. well, maybe
    c. it all depends
    d. kids in church are some of the worst at taking advantage of you

Mid-Course Affirmation

Introduction. It's half time. Time for a break. Get together with your team of 8 (or the whole group if you have less than twelve) and evaluate your experience so far.

Here are two options. The second option is more risky, but a lot more personal if you have grown to appreciate each other.

Option 1: Half-time Progress Report. Turn to page three and let everyone report any growth in your life since being in this program.

Option 2: Appreciation Time. Ask one person on your team to sit in silence while the others share one thing that you have come to appreciate about this person. Finish one of these sentences:

Since being in your group, I have come to see you as. . .

or

Since being in your group, I have come to appreciate you for your. . .

After you have gone around your group on the first person, ask the next person to sit in silence while the others finish the sentence on this person. . .etc. around the group.

This is called "strength bombardment" or "appreciation bombardment." You've done a lot of talking about yourself during this program. Now you will have a chance to hear what the others on your team have learned about you. Get set for a beautiful experience in AFFIRMATION.

If you don't know how to get started, look over the list below and pick out a word or two words that help describe what you see in this person. . .and tell them so.

I SEE YOU AS VERY. . . :

loyal	quiet	dependable	daring
fun	gorgeous	resourceful	lovable
friendly	childlike	cheerful	steady
irresistible	sensitive	meditative	spiritual
caring	unsinkable	warm	dedicated
gentle	rugged	awesome	emerging
strong	untamed	playful	crazy
courageous	special	thoughtful	energetic
encouraging	beautiful	persistent	confident

SESSION 5 - COACH'S BOX

GAME PLAN: Getting Personal. At the end of this session, the group will be introduced to a form of shared prayer—based on prayer requests. On the disclosure scale, this session will be medium to high risk.

ON THE DISCLOSURE SCALE: Session 5

No Risk_____x_____High Risk

AGENDA/FORMAT: Four parts to the meeting. Chairs are rearranged for each step in the agenda.

STEP 1:	**STEP 2:**	**STEP 3:**	**STEP 4:**
Crowd Breaker	**Warm Up**	**Bible Study**	**Caring**
All together or	Groups of 2	Groups of 4	Teams of 8
Teams of 8	15 minutes	15-30 minutes	15-20 minutes
15 minutes			

CROWD BREAKERS/15 Minutes

King of the Ring: Take a piece of chalk, or, better yet, a rope and make a circle approximately four feet wide. Have the group (or two volunteers from each small group) stand inside the circle. ASK everyone to hold their left foot behind their back with their right hand. When the whistle blows, you try to bump the others out of the circle. Anyone who steps on the chalk line or the rope is out. When most of the people are eliminated, blow the whistle and have the group stop. Shorten the circle and "battle till the death." Have a separate contest for girls and boys. Scoring: 3,000 points for first place; 2,000 for second; 1,000 for third.

Arm Wrestling: Have playoffs to see who is the best at arm wrestling.

Breath Contest: The winner is the person who can talk the longest without stopping for a breath.

Spelling Bee: Have the group line up and find a difficult word in the dictionary for each person. Score as before the first, second and third place finishers.

Laughing Contest: The point of this contest is to see who can keep a straight face. Choose one of the class members to be the clown, trying to get the rest of the class to laugh. The winner is the one who keeps a straight face the longest. The only rule is that the clown must maintain a distance of at least four feet from the class member. Reward points as mentioned above.

SESSION 5
Making It Right

Decorating My Life

Introduction. This begins the second half of this program. Up to now, you have been dealing with the little hassles in your life. Now, we will start dealing with the big hassles.

To get started, think of your life right now like a house—and the various rooms in the house like the various areas of your life.

Get together with one other person from your team and choose a good poster for each room in your life. Explain to your partner why this would be a good poster for that room. Then reverse the roles and let your partner choose posters for their life.

- ❑ LIVING ROOM: My lifestyle, my values, my moral principles
- ❑ RECREATION ROOM: My leisure time, priorities, activities
- ❑ FAMILY ROOM: My relationships with parents, brothers/sisters
- ❑ LIBRARY ROOM: My reading habits, music, mind-control
- ❑ PHYSICAL FITNESS ROOM: My body, keeping in shape
- ❑ GUEST ROOM: My friends, schoolmates, concern for others

1. Be patient, God isn't finished with me yet.
2. Are we there yet?
3. Hang in there!
4. Nowhere to go but up!
5. Have a nice day someplace else.
6. Outta my way, I'm goin' for it.
7. Music speaks when words cannot.
8. Winning isn't everything. It is the only thing.
9. Love is patient and kind.
10. There is light at the end of the tunnel. I hope it is not a train.
11. Fragile: Handle with care.
12. I am easy to please as long as I have things my way.
13. Christians aren't perfect: Just forgiven.
14. What would Jesus do?
15. Some days the windshield. Some days the bug.
16. All things are possible through Christ.
17. Nobody loves me but my mama. And she may be lying, too.

Mending Our Fences

Introduction. What do you do when a relationship gets bad—really bad. Jesus gave some pretty clear instructions to his followers on what to do.

Listen to his teaching on anger and broken relationships. Then, move into groups of four and discuss the questionnaire. Be sure to save the last 20 minutes at the close for the Caring time.

TEACHING ABOUT ANGER

[21] *"You have heard that people were told in the past, 'Do not commit murder; anyone who does will be brought to trial.'* [22]*But now I tell you: if you are angry with your brother you will be brought to trial, if you call your brother 'You good-for-nothing!' you will be brought before the Council, and if you call your brother a worthless fool you will be in danger of going to the fire of hell.* [23]*So if you are about to offer your gift to God at the altar and there you remember that your brother has something against you,* [24]*leave your gift there in front of the altar, go at once and make peace with your brother, and then come back and offer your gift to God.*

[25]*"If someone brings a lawsuit against you and takes you to court, settle the dispute while there is time, before you get to court. Once you are there, you will be turned over to the judge, who will hand you over to the police, and you will be put in jail.* [26]*There you will stay, I tell you, until you pay the last penny of your fine."*

Matthew 5:21-26

Looking Into The Story: In groups of four, let one person answer question #1, the next person question #2, etc. Remember, there are no right or wrong answers. If you disagree with what has been said, speak up.

1. What was your first thought as you heard this scripture teaching from Jesus?
   a. I knew that I should have stayed home today
   b. this is going to be another boring Bible study
   c. I'm not going to do that
   d. I think about that broken relationship every time I go to church
   e. I wish I could do this, but I can't
   f. this sounds like a pansy
   g. other:_____

2. From what Jesus says about murder, what do you think was going on in his group of followers?
   a. they must have been killing each other
   b. they probably were picking on someone in the group
   c. they probably enjoyed putting each other down—like people will do
   d. they must have taken someone to court
   e. they must have had a big fight in the group

3. What is the principle here on dealing with an enemy?
   a. lay down and let them walk over you
   b. make them come and make it right
   c. you go to them and have it out
   d. get a third party to listen to both of you
   e. smear their reputation any way you can

4. What is Jesus talking about when he says: "Leave your gift there in front of the altar, go at once and make peace with your brother"?
   a. I'm not sure
   b. he wants me to crawl back to the person that has hurt me and let him hurt me again
   c. he expects me to say "I'm sorry" when I'm not
   d. take a "peace offering" to my brother

My Own Story: Discuss the CASE STUDY first. Then, move to the questions under Reflection and share your own experience.

CASE STUDY: Mary and her Dad
Mary's parents got a divorce when she was seven years old. Her dad moved to an apartment and later remarried. Mary spent every other weekend with her dad, but she had trouble getting along with his new wife..Her dad loves her very much, but he is an engineer and finds it difficult showing his feelings. When he moved to Seattle, the "visiting privileges" stopped, and Mary lost contact with her dad. Last week, Mary's dad called to ask if she would like to come to Seattle for Christmas. She has all sorts of mixed feelings about her dad, his new wife, and herself.

1. If you were Mary, what would you do?
   a. make some excuse for not going
   b. tell him out right that you do not want to spend Christmas with him
   c. let your mother explain
   d. write him a long letter yourself, explaining why you do not want to see him
   e. go ahead and spend Christmas with him, but keep quiet about your feelings
   f. other:_____

2. If you were Mary, how would you deal with his new wife if you came to visit?
   a. have nothing to do with her
   b. sit down with both of them and tell them exactly how you feel
   c. take his new wife out for a private talk
   d. try to act pleasant and say nothing
   e. take a friend along that you can be with and avoid the situation
   f. sweep the whole thing under the rug
   g. other:_____

Reflection: Go around on the first question and let everyone answer the question. Then, go around again for the second question, etc.

1. If you had to give yourself a grade on dealing with broken relationships in a constructive and timely manner, what would the grade be?
   a. I'm going to give myself an A+ on this
   b. B+ for trying
   c. C+ for putting it off
   d. I'm getting better

2. What relationship in your life do you find it the hardest to deal with?
   a. my parent
   b. my brother/sister
   c. my close friends
   d. my boyfriend/girlfriend
   e. my teachers/coaches
   f. my boss
   g. my youth group

3. When a relationship has turned sour, who do you turn to for help or to talk it over?
   a. a close friend
   b. my parent
   c. my youth leader
   d. no one

4. What have you found very helpful in dealing with a broken relationship?
   a. writing a letter
   b. asking the person out for a coke
   c. taking the person to a movie or ball game
   d. sending flowers
   e. trying to be extra nice
   f. staying out of their way
   g. asking someone else to speak to the person for you
   h. forgetting it. . .and getting on with life
   i. other:_____

5. In your youth group, how are you in dealing with broken relationships?
   a. denial—we have never had a broken relationship
   b. silence—we don't talk about it
   c. prayer—we get God involved
   d. second-hand information—some how the youth leaders hear about it—and they bring it up
   e. direct assault—head on
   f. once a year—at the youth retreat, we make up

Getting Personal

Introduction. Here are two options to close the session on problems.

Option 1: Follow the usual procedure. Regather as teams and report-in on the session—what you learned—and spend some time in prayer with your prayer partner.

Option 2: Try a new form of sharing prayer requests and praying for one another. If you choose this option, here are the instructions.

1. Get together in groups of three.

2. Let one person share a prayer request by answering the question:

> *How can we help you in prayer this week?*

3. The other two in the three-some respond to this prayer request in this way:

- One person prays a prayer of THANKS. . .

    "God, I want to THANK YOU for (name). . . ."

- The other person prays a prayer of PETITION. . .

    "God, I ask your help for my friend (name), for. . . ."

4. When you have finished with the first person, let the next person share a request and the other two pray for this person, etc. . . around the group of three.

Remember, in your group of three, you start out by letting one person answer this question:

> *How can we help you in prayer this week?*

SESSION 6 - COACH'S BOX

GAME PLAN: Learning to Care. At the end of this session, the group members will be invited to share their needs and to reach out and care for one another. On the disclosure scale, this session will be high risk.

ON THE DISCLOSURE SCALE: Session 6.
No Risk_____x___High Risk

AGENDA/FORMAT: Four parts to the meeting. Chairs are rearranged for each step in the agenda.

STEP 1: Crowd Breaker All together or Teams of 8 15 minutes	STEP 2: Warm Up Groups of 2 15 minutes	STEP 3: Bible Study Groups of 4 15-30 minutes	STEP 4: Caring Teams of 8 15-20 minutes

CROWD BREAKERS/15 Minutes

Guess Who/Charades

This crowd breaker is great for a small group to compete against other small groups. Before the session, prepare a set of 8 stick-on name tags for each small group. The name tags can be: movie stars, well-known athletes, comic strip of fictional characters—anyone that can be easily and quickly portrayed. While the Leader is explaining the directions, have two helpers go to the small groups and put the name tags on each person—a different tag for every one in the group.

On the word GO, one person in each small group turns around and lets the others in the small group see the name tag on his or her back. Then, the others start acting out (in silence) this character until the person can guess who it is.

Then the second person in the small group turns around and lets the others see the name tag. The others act out this character until the person can guess who it is, etc., until everyone in the group has guessed. The first small group to guess all the characters wins.

Dog-Patch Olympics
- ❏ 200-foot crawl relay (4 team members crawling 50 feet backwards—on all fours—carrying the baton—toilet roll—in their mouth)
- ❏ Potato sack hop relay (4 on each team)
- ❏ Egg toss (winner is twosome that throws farthest distance to partner without breaking egg)
- ❏ Piggyback relay
- ❏ Wheelbarrow race relay
- ❏ Discus throw (paper plate)
- ❏ Javelin (plastic straws)

Each team has to enter one or more people in each event. Winner of each event gets 10 points

SESSION 6
The God of Surprises

Super Bowl Party

Introduction. This is the next to last session in this program on hassles. You have talked a lot about hassles. Now, in this session, you will have a chance to talk about the standard for healthy relationships in the Bible.

To get started, get together with one person that you have not been with before and have fun creating a fantasy Super Bowl Party for your youth group. Let your partner ask you the questions below and serve as your secretary as you outline your party. Then, let them report back with the two half-finished sentences at the bottom under FEEDBACK.

Then, reverse the roles and let your partner plan their party.

1. If you had a budget of $1,000, where would you like to have a party for your youth group?

2. What kind of decorations would you have?

3. What are you going to serve?

4. What music group would you like to bring? What special songs are you going to ask them to perform?

5. What other kinds of entertainment are you going to have?

6. How will you ask the people to dress?

7. Will there be any special party gifts?

8. What special guests are you going to invite?

9. What other youth groups would you like to invite?

10. What little surprise would you like to have at the party?

FEEDBACK: Let your partner reply by finishing these two sentences:
1. The thing I like most about your party plan is. . .

2. If I could bring a friend to this party, I would like to bring. . .

On the Road Again

Introduction. You have dealt with every kind of hassle in your life except the most difficult—the hassle with yourself. This is especially hard when it comes to disappointment and personal failure.

In this Bible study, we want you to listen to the experience of two followers of Jesus who have lost hope and decided to throw in the towel. It is right after the resurrection of Jesus. But these two followers have chosen not to believe the news. Instead, they have decided to leave town.

Listen in on their conversation as Jesus sneaks up on them and lets them talk about their disappointment. Then, move quickly into groups of four and discuss the questionnaire.

Be sure to save at least 30 minutes at the close to evaluate this program with your entire team. . . .and to decide what you are going to do next.

THE WALK TO EMMAUS

¹³On that same day two of Jesus' followers were going to a village named Emmaus, about seven miles from Jerusalem, ¹⁴and they were talking to each other about all the things that had happened. ¹⁵As they talked and discussed, Jesus himself drew near and walked along with them; ¹⁶they saw him, but somehow did not recognize him. ¹⁷Jesus said to them, "What are you talking about to each other, as you walk along?"

They stood still, with sad faces. ¹⁸One of them, named Cleopas, asked him, "Are you the only visitor in Jerusalem who doesn't know the things that have been happening there these last few days?"

¹⁹"What things?" he asked.

"The things that happened to Jesus of Nazareth," they answered. "This man was a prophet and was considered by God and by all the people to be powerful in everything he said and did. ²⁰Our chief priests and rulers handed him over to be sentenced to death, and he was crucified. ²¹And we had hoped that he would be the one who was going to set Israel free! Besides all that, this is now the third day since it happened. ²²Some of the women of our group surprised us; they went at dawn to the tomb, ²³but could not find his body. They came back saying they had seen a vision of angels who told them that he is alive. ²⁴Some of our group went to the tomb and found it exactly as the women had said, but they did not see him."

²⁵Then Jesus said to them, "How foolish you are, how slow you are to believe everything the prophets said! ²⁶Was it not necessary for the Messiah to suffer these things and then to enter his glory?" ²⁷And Jesus explained to them what was said about himself in all the Scriptures, beginning with the books of Moses and the writings of all the prophets.

²⁸As they came near the village to which they were going, Jesus acted as if he were going farther; ²⁹but they held him back, saying, "Stay with us; the day is almost over and it is getting dark." So he went in to stay with them. ³⁰He sat down to eat with them, took the bread, and said the blessing; then he broke the bread and gave it to them. ³¹Then their eyes were opened and they recognized him, but he disappeared from their sight. ³²They said to each other, "Wasn't it like a fire burning in us when he talked to us on the road and explained the Scriptures to us?"

³³They got up at once and went back to Jerusalem, where they found the eleven disciples gathered together with the others ³⁴and saying, "The Lord is risen indeed! He has appeared to Simon!"

³⁵The two then explained to them what had happened on the road, and how they had recognized the Lord when he broke the bread.

Luke 24:13-35

Looking Into The Story: In groups of 4, let one person answer question #1, the next person question #2, etc.

1. Why do you think these two guys left town?
   a. fear—they were afraid for their lives
   b. disillusionment—the suffering and crucifixion of Christ wiped them out
   c. shame—they were ashamed of their non-belief
   d. doubt—they didn't believe that Jesus had really come back from the dead
   e. loneliness—they wanted to get back home
   f. other:_____

2. If you had been Jesus, would you have chased down these two run-aways?
   a. no, let them go. They don't deserve to be a part of the team
   b. well, I might give them one more chance
   c. sure, that is what Jesus is all about

3. After they pulled this stunt, would you let them back into your youth group?
   a. no, we don't allow non-believers in our group
   b. well, we might take them back on probation
   c. sure, if they promised never to do this again
   d. we are all clowns—on our way back to God—these two would be right at home

4. When do you think these two clowns found faith?
   a. when they started to unpack their sad story
   b. when Jesus explained to them the scripture
   c. when their heart started to "burn"
   d. when they got back to the group and told the group what had happened
   e. when the group accepted them back

My Own Story: This is the last sharing time in this program. Use this opportunity to talk about your own "journey home". Go around the group on question #1. Then, go around on question #2, etc. through the questions.

1. What is the closest you have come to "throwing in the towel" and leaving the church?
   a. when I got jilted
   b. when my friend died
   c. when I got away from church
   d. years ago
   e. recently
   f. I never have

2. What was it that brought you back to faith?
   a. healing from a hurt
   b. slowly—new life started to happen
   c. taking time to be with God
   d. getting back into the scripture
   e. being with Christian friends
   f. other:_____

3. What did you learn during that time you were away from God?
   a. it's lonely out there
   b. God never lets you alone
   c. it's OK to struggle
   d. once you've given your heart to God, God is going to be more visible
   e. there is always a way home

4. How would you describe your relationship with God right now?
   a. up and down
   b. growing
   c. going steady
   d. slipping
   e. blah
   f. exciting
   g. other:_____

5. What has been the most exciting thing to happen recently in your relationship with God?
   a. getting to know God in a personal way
   b. learning to pray
   c. discovering Christian community—around Christ
   d. finding out I am not alone in my problems
   e. studying the Bible
   f. sharing my faith
   g. other:_____

Learning to Care

Introduction: You are nearly through with this course as a youth group. Next week, you will have a chance to celebrate and decide what you are going to do next.

   To prepare for your last session together, take a few minutes right now and reflect on what and where you have changed during this course. If you have stayed with the same team throughout this course, you will be able to say how you have seen your teammates change. If you don't know each other that well, you will do the talking for yourself. Here are two steps to follow.

1. **Affirmation.** Go around and let everyone on your team answer one or more of the questions below. Again, if you know each other, use this opportunity to share how you have seen your teammates grow.

   • Where have you grown in your own life during this course?
   • Where have you seen growth in some of the others in your group during this course?
   • What have you appreciated most about the group during this course?

2. **Option.** At this point, your team can choose one of two ways to close the meeting.

   • **Option 1: Prayer Partners.** Get together with your prayer partner and report on your week. Then close in prayer.

   • **Option 2: Circle of Love.** Stay together with your team and express your feelings for each other non-verbally. Here is how. Follow carefully:

   a. Stand in a circle—about a foot apart
   b. Everyone puts their right hand in front of them—palm up
   c. Team leader steps into the circle and goes to one person. Looks them in the eyes for a few seconds. Then, takes their hand and tries to express the care you feel for this person by doing something to their hand—such as gripping it firmly, stroking it, shaking it. . .etc. Use only appropriate gestures.
   d. After the Team Leader has gone around the circle, the next person goes around the circle in the same way, etc. . . until everyone has gone around the circle.
   Remember, all of this is done <u>without words.</u>

         BUT IN SHAKING THE HANDS OF THOSE IN YOUR
         GROUP, YOU CAN SAY A LOT—HOW YOU CARE!

SESSION 7 - COACH'S BOX

GAME PLAN: Team Celebration. At the close of this session, you can have a special worship service (see below) or a party to evaluate and celebrate your experience as a team. On the disclosure scale, this session will be no risk to high risk, depending on what you choose.

> ON THE DISCLOSURE SCALE: Session 7
> No Risk_x_____x_High Risk

AGENDA/FORMAT: Four parts to the meeting. Chairs are rearranged for each step in the agenda.

STEP 1:	STEP 2:	STEP 3:	STEP 4:
Crowd Breaker	**Warm Up**	**Bible Study**	**Caring**
All together or	Groups of 2	Groups of 4	Teams of 8
Teams of 8	15 minutes	15-30 minutes	15-20 minutes
15 minutes			

CROWD BREAKER/15 Minutes.

Ice Cream Special

This game is for those who love to make and eat ice cream sundaes. Kids pair off and create one sundae for each couple. No skimping on those gooey toppings.

Now the race begins. Couples lie on the floor in a straight line on their backs with their heads touching. All heads must remain flat on the floor. The first couple to consume their sundae (with more inside them than on them!) wins the race.

And don't forget to reward your winners with a gift certificate to an ice cream parlor.*

SERENDIPITY SERVICE/30 minutes. A Caring time closing exercise for the whole youth group. If you choose to use this activity, allow enough time. You may have to shorten other parts of the meeting.

Use a quiet meditative place for this time where students can worship and share how God has worked in their lives in the past weeks. A prayer room, fireside, candlelight in your regular room, etc. will help make this a unique experience. Introduce a period of sharing by leading the group in some worship songs and then have each of them explain what God is asking them to do or the next move in their lives in light of what they have learned and experienced. Then have that person kneel or sit in the center of the group while the others reach in to touch and pray for this person to do as God is leading them. Let one person voice the prayer for the whole group. Continue until each person has shared and been commissioned to move forward with God.

*Reprinted with permission from Group Publishing.

SESSION 7
High Octane Love

Fun Affirmation

Introduction. Instead of the usual Warm Up exercise, we suggest that you devote 5 minutes right now to preparation for the Wrap Up experience at the close of this session.

Get together with the team that you have been with through this program and sit quietly for five minutes as you look over the list of comic strip and famous people below. Jot down the initials of the members of your team next to the comic strip character or famous person that your teammate reminds you of. For instance, you might put Bill's initials next to Big Bird, because Bill reminds you of Big Bird.

Do not tell anyone what you have done. Just make your selections and wait until the closing exercise to share.

___ Tom Cruise	___ Whoopie Goldberg
___ Arnold Schwarzenegger	___ Tom Hanks
___ Christie Brinkley	___ Michael Jordan
___ Ken Griffey, Jr.	___ Julia Roberts
___ David Letterman	___ Charlie Brown
___ Snoopy	___ Schroeder
___ Garfield	___ Gloria Estefan
___ Robin Williams	___ The Beauty
___ Mariah Carey	___ The Beast
___ Batman	___ Troy Aikman
___ Kermit	___ Tina Turner
___ Janet Jackson	___ Superman
___ Fred Flintstone	___ Lois Lane
___ Wilma Flintstone	___ Other:_____

Love Is. . .

Introduction. This program on hassles would not be complete without a session on love. And the best passage in the Bible about love is the Love Chapter—1 Corinthians 13.

Instead of the usual Bible discussion, we are going to give you a self-grading test to see how you would compare yourself to the standard of love in this passage.

After someone has read the Bible passage, move into groups of four and let one person in your group read the first phrase of this passage. Then, go around your group and let everyone give a number between 1 and 10—1 being SUPER LOW and 10 being SUPER HIGH in that area.

Then, read the next phrase and go around again, etc. until you have worked through the entire passage.

If you have time left over, move to the REFLECTION questions.

LOVE

⁴Love is patient and kind; it is not jealous or conceited or proud; ⁵love is not ill-mannered or selfish or irritable; love does not keep a record of wrongs; ⁶love is not happy with evil, but is happy with the truth. ⁷Love never gives up; and its faith, hope, and patience never fail.   1 Corinthians 13:4-7

Love is patient: I don't take out my frustrations on those I love. I am calm under pressure and careful with my tongue.

TOTAL FAILURE   1 2 3 4 5 6 7 8 9 10   A SUCCESS

Love is kind: I think before I act, especially with those I love. I cushion anything I say with prayer and consideration.

TOTAL FAILURE   1 2 3 4 5 6 7 8 9 10   A SUCCESS

Love is not jealous: I am not jealous of my time when those I love need me or want me to do something special.

TOTAL FAILURE   1 2 3 4 5 6 7 8 9 10   A SUCCESS

Love is not conceited: I don't consider my role any more important than those I love—or talk like "I know better."

TOTAL FAILURE   1 2 3 4 5 6 7 8 9 10   A SUCCESS

Love is not proud: I don't think of myself as better than those I love; or better at sports. . .or singing. . .or handling money.

TOTAL FAILURE 1 2 3 4 5 6 7 8 9 10 A SUCCESS

Love is not ill-mannered: I don't make cutting or crude remarks when I don't get my way—or become silent and withdrawn.

TOTAL FAILURE 1 2 3 4 5 6 7 8 9 10 A SUCCESS

Love is not selfish: I don't put myself first. I try to think of those I love for spiritual and emotional support.

TOTAL FAILURE 1 2 3 4 5 6 7 8 9 10 A SUCCESS

Love is not irritable: I don't let little things bother me, especially with those I love. I have a muffler on my mouth.

TOTAL FAILURE 1 2 3 4 5 6 7 8 9 10 A SUCCESS

Love does not keep a record of wrongs: I don't keep score of the number of times those I love have said something or done something that upset me, and I don't bring it up when we have a new disagreement.

TOTAL FAILURE 1 2 3 4 5 6 7 8 9 10 A SUCCESS

Love is not happy with evil: There is a difference between acceptance and approval. I accept those I love, but I do not have to approve of everything they do.

TOTAL FAILURE 1 2 3 4 5 6 7 8 9 10 A SUCCESS

Love is happy with the truth: I am filled with joy when I think that God is working out his perfect plan for those I love—to make these people fully mature in Christ. . .one day.

TOTAL FAILURE 1 2 3 4 5 6 7 8 9 10 A SUCCESS

Love never gives up: I am always there for those I love—even when they upset me—seeking to comfort and care as Christ would.

TOTAL FAILURE 1 2 3 4 5 6 7 8 9 10 A SUCCESS

Love always trusts: I believe in those I love and I believe in God. And I am willing to let God do the shaping and molding.

TOTAL FAILURE 1 2 3 4 5 6 7 8 9 10 A SUCCESS

Love always hopes: I am good at expecting the best and thinking the best about those I love. I always give those I love the benefit of the doubt.

TOTAL FAILURE 1 2 3 4 5 6 7 8 9 10 A SUCCESS

Love always perseveres: I am committed to those I love and I am prepared to see it through to the end.

TOTAL FAILURE 1 2 3 4 5 6 7 8 9 10 A SUCCESS

REFLECTION: Go around on the first question and let everyone explain their answer. Then, go around again on the second question, etc. . .through the questions.

1. How do you feel after taking this love inventory on your life?
   a. like crawling into a hole
   b. like giving up
   c. like trying harder
   d. like: _____

2. Without putting yourself down, what area of your love life do you need to work on the most?
   a. my family
   b. my close friends
   c. my teammates/school mates
   d. my relationship with myself

3. What could the youth group do to encourage you in this?
   a. hold me accountable
   b. encourage me
   c. pray for me
   d. give me a pat on the back once in a while
   e. let me be
   f. other:_____

What Happened?

Introduction: You have two options for this special closing experience: (1) The worship service described in the Coach's Box, or (2) A de-briefing session, using the agenda below.

1. **Warm Up Exercise:** Regather as teams (or the entire youth group together) and share the results of the Warm Up exercise. Ask one person to sit in silence while everyone on their team explains where they have put this person's name and why. Then, move to the next person, etc. around the group. Use this opportunity to share your appreciation for the contributions you have made to each other in the team.

2. **Evaluation:** Go around on the first question below and let everyone explain their answer. Then, go around again on the next question, etc.

   A. When you first started on this course, what did you think about it?
   a. I liked it
   b. I had some reservations
   c. I only came for the fun
   d. I was bored
   e. other:_____

   B. How would you describe the experience of opening up and sharing your ideas and problems with this group?
   a. scary
   b. very difficult
   c. exciting
   d. a life-changing experience
   e. invaluable
   f. okay, but. . .
   g. just what I needed
   h. a beautiful breakthrough

   C. What was the high point in this program for you?
   a. fun
   b. times of prayer
   c. feeling of belonging to others who really care
   d. being with teammates who are committed to Christ
   e. knowing I am not alone in my problems
   f. finding myself again
   g. Bible study
   h. learning to deal with my hang-ups

3. **Personal Change.** Turn back to page 3 and let everyone explain where they have changed during this course.

4. **What's Next.** As a group, decide what you are going to do next.

A Word To The Youth Leaders

Congratulations. You are working with the most potential-packed audience in the world—Teenagers. This is one of the most difficult times in their lives. They are making big decisions, often alone or in packs. Peers are important to them and there is tremendous pressure to do what peers demand and the chance to think critically about choices. This youth program is designed to give teenagers a feeling of belonging. A family of peers. An alternative to the gang at school. Or an alternative inside of the school.

This program is built around the idea of teamwork. The goal is to help youth "bring out the best in one another." By agreeing on a set of goals. Agreeing on a level of commitment for a period of time (seven weeks). By setting ground rules, and holding each other accountable. If this sounds like something out of educational psychology, it is. The dynamics are the same. The only difference is the motive and the learning objective. The goal of this program is spiritual formation. Christian orientation. Christian value clarification. Christian moral development. Christian commitment.

The Importance Of Voluntary Commitment

The difference between this program and the typical youth program in the church is the commitment level. To get into this program, a youth *must* commit himself or herself to being in the program. This means "choosing" to be in the program every session for seven weeks, to be a team player in order to make the group process work.

Anyone who has been involved in team sports will understand this principle. And anyone who has coached a team will understand the role of the student pastor or youth leader. The youth leader is the coach and the youth group is the squad. And the squad is broken up into small units or teams of six to eight—with a sub-coach or facilitator inside of each team.

Structure Of The Youth Meetings

The meetings look like typical training workouts of a sports camp. First, the whole squad meets together for some limbering up exercises (all together or by teams of eight competing against one another if you have a large youth group). Then, the entire squad pairs off for some basic, one-on-one "conversation starters" to break the ice. Then, with your partner, groups of four are formed for the Bible Study discussion. Finally, the team of eight is regathered for a little wrap-up and caring for each other. The typical meeting looks like this:

Step 1:	**Step 2:**	**Step 3:**	**Step 4:**
Crowd Breaker	Conversation	Bible Study/	Wrap Up and
Team of 8	Starters/	Groups of 4	Caring/
or all together	Groups of 2	or half of team	Teams of 8

Moving from the large group (Step 1) to groups of two (Step 2) to groups of 4 (Step 3) to groups of 8 (Step 4) will not only offer a spontaneity to the meeting, but will also position the youth to be in the best size of group for the particular type of activity.

Step 1:	**Step 2:**	**Step 3:**	**Step 4:**
Purpose: To kick off the meeting.	Purpose: To start a relationship	Purpose: To discuss Bible Story	Purpose: To care for one another.

In the first session in this course, the ideal would be to form teams of eight that can stay together for the entire course. This could be done by random selection or by designating the teams to break up cliques. Or it can be done in a serendipitous fashion by giving out slips of song titles and having the youth find out who is on their team by whistling their song until they "find each other." For junior highs, we recommend that an adult or older youth be in each team of eight.

If you only have fifteen or twenty youth in your entire group, you could keep all of the squad together for Step 1 and Step 4, and break into 2's and 4's for Step 2 and Step 3.

In Case of Emergency, Read the Instructions

In the margin beside each Step, you will find instructions to the leader. Read this. Sometimes, the instructions are important. Trust us. We have written this program based on our experience. Give the program a chance. There is method to the madness. Particularly, the fast-paced movement from 2's to 4's to 8's.

Get a commitment out of your youth before you start the program for seven weeks or seven sessions. And remind them (by thanking them every week) for making this commitment.Here's to the thing that God is about to do in your youth. Here's to the future of your church—your youth.

Serendipity House is a publisher specializing in small groups. Serendipity has been providing training and resources for youth ministry for over 30 years. As we continue to develop materials for youth groups, we would love to hear your comments, ideas or suggestions. Call us at 1-800-525-9563.

**ABOUT
LYMAN COLEMAN
THE AUTHOR**

The Serendipity Youth Bible Study Series is the culmination of forty years in youth ministry for Lyman Coleman, the author of the series.

Lyman Coleman started out in youth work in the 50's with Young Life while he was a student at Baylor University in Texas, and with the Navigators while doing graduate work at Biblical Seminary in New York and New York University.

In the 60's, he pioneered a variety of team-building programs for youth that combined group work with outreach missions: the coffee house (*The Coffee House Itch*), folk musicals (*Man Alive*), film making (*Festival*), and multi-media happenings *(Kaleidoscope)*.

In the 70's, he integrated the strategies of values clarification, moral development and interactive Bible study in a series of youth courses for Word Books entitled *The Serendipity Youth Series.* He also created the special huddle programs for the Fellowship of Christian Athletes and parent courses for World Wide Marriage Encounter (*Evenings for Couples* and *Evenings for Parents).*

In the 80's, he collaborated with Denny Rydberg (President of Young Life) in a series of youth Bible study courses covering the felt needs of youth. He also was the general editor of the *Serendipity Bible for Groups.*

In the 90's he designed the scope and sequence library of resources for spiritual formation in the church through elective support groups covering all levels of spiritual formation—in which the *Youth Bible Study Series* is a part.

Hundreds of youth workers have contributed their ideas and dozens of youth leaders have had a part in the writing in the formative years, especially David Stone, Don Kimball, Dr. Richard Peace, Denny Rydberg, Keith Madsen and the Serendipity Staff.

Lyman lives in Littleton, Colorado, with his wife, Margaret, and three grown children and their families.

**SERENDIPITY
HOUSE**

SERENDIPITY HOUSE is a publishing house that creates programs like this one for many types of groups in the church: kick off groups, Bible study groups, support groups, recovery groups and mission/task groups. The philosophy behind these groups is the same: (1) help the group agree upon the purpose and ground rules, (2) spend the first few sessions you are together getting acquainted, (3) shift gears in Bible study as the group matures, and (4) help the group say "goodbye" and decompress when they are through with their purpose.